Phillip & Familia~

May this cocktail book
bring you lots of fu...

Yvette

VIANNEY RODRIGUEZ & YVETTE MARQUEZ-SHARPNACK

LATIN TWIST

TRADITIONAL & MODERN COCKTAILS

PHOTOGRAPHY BY JEANINE THURSTON

Hippocrene Books
New York

Color photographs: Jeanine Thurston
Illustrations: Brittany Hince
Book and jacket design: Heidi Larsen
Design editor: Yvette Marquez-Sharpnack

For more information, address:
HIPPOCRENE BOOKS, INC.
171 Madison Avenue
New York, NY 10016
www.hippocrenebooks.com

Library of Congress Cataloging-in-Publication Data

Marquez-Sharpnack, Yvette.
    Latin Twist : Traditional & Modern Cocktails / Yvette Marquez-Sharpnack and
Vianney Rodriguez; photography by Jeanine Thurston.
    pages cm
    Includes index.
    ISBN 978-0-7818-1342-6 (hardcover) -- ISBN 0-7818-1342-5 (hardcover)
1. Cocktails--Latin America. I. Rodriguez, Vianney. II. Title.
    TX951.M268 2015
    641.598--dc23
                    2014050207

Printed in the United States of America.

To our blog readers and online friends who continuously
support our love of food and cocktails.
This book is dedicated to everyone who enjoys
sipping, shaking, mixing, and entertaining.
We hope you are inspired to host a fiesta and create beautiful
exotic cocktails for your family and friends.
Salud!

CONTENTS

This book is about celebrating Latin cultures.

Being of Mexican descent we are very familiar with popular Mexican cocktails like Margaritas and Piña Coladas, but what has been exciting and rewarding about writing this book is learning about the luscious variety of cocktails from other Latin American countries.

Cocktail recipes can go in and out of style, but it is so gratifying to see that classic treasures from Latin American countries are enjoyed at bars and tables around the world now. For example, a Cuba Libre or a Caipirinha from Brazil can be found at most bars these days. If you haven't tried these classics yet, believe us you will want to! We researched many varieties and recipes and share the best ones here with you.

We both love to entertain and delight in mixing up new cocktails for our guests. With *Latin Twist* we invite you to share our love of spirits and gatherings with family and friends while discovering traditional and modern drinks you will love.

This collection of cocktails represents a sampling of what Latin America has to offer. It's a great way to start what we hope will be a lifelong adventure in exploring new drinks and flavors. We are not mixologists or bartenders; we are simply Latinas who appreciate a delicious cocktail and the story behind it. Beyond the flavor profiles, the alcohol varieties, the chemical interactions, the endless recipes and mixers, it is this history that keeps us fascinated.

These recipes do not take hours to make, and almost all of the ingredients are readily available. But never fear, we share substitution suggestions when needed. We also have options to make larger quantities so you can enjoy your fiesta without working a cocktail shaker the whole night.

Invite some guests over, raise a glass, and celebrate with a *Latin Twist*.

CHEERS, SALUD, SAÚDE!

Ever since I can remember, cocktails have always had a place at our family festivities. We didn't have birthday parties for children at the local pizza joint—we had a backyard fiesta with lots of cousins and a piñata. The kids played all day, while the adults enjoyed their drinks and caught up on the latest *chisme* (gossip) into the night. I still remember the musical sound of laughter as the women sat with their cocktails and reminisced. When I was a little girl I used to play bartender. I'd see who had an empty can or glass and get them a fresh cold beer or make them a Cuba Libre (rum and coke with a twist of lime). The more alcohol served, the longer the party would last! It was simple math—if I wanted to play with my cousins as long as I could, that meant keeping the grownups busy drinking.

Today my family still celebrates in the same style. Our parties are filled with family and friends, lots of delicious food, and of course, cocktails. If I'm hosting a celebration in our home, I love to prepare a themed drink to serve. Mexican Sangria for fall and winter, Cheladas for a spicy dinner, or Palomas for a casual summer gathering. For the most part, my cocktails are Mexican drinks—I grew up savoring Mexican flavors so it's what I know and what's in my blood.

Writing *Latin Twist* has opened my eyes to the many varieties of Latin American beverages. No matter where you start—with an Argentine Calipso, a Peruvian Pisco Sour, or any of the other refreshing cocktails—through this book I am excited to share with you a Latin cocktail journey of exotic flavors and combinations.

Yvette

Growing up, I knew my mom was the ultimate hostess; she would wake up early and head right to the kitchen to prepare an elaborate feast for her guests. She was a whiz in the kitchen, able to whip up a meal out of practically nothing if a family member or friend should happen to stop in. Her talent in the kitchen made our home the central location for many family celebrations. My dad (Papi) was in charge of the grill, entertaining the guests outdoors and keeping everyone in lively spirits. He stocked bottles of liquor under the kitchen sink and his makeshift bar was always ready for a fiesta.

Even though I was quite young, I knew exactly how to prepare Papi's tequila, how to properly serve chilled beer in his favorite glass, and how to work the crowd graciously, asking if anyone needed a refill or wanted something special to drink. Most importantly, I knew to always, always check in with my beloved *abuelita*, who despite being a fierce spirit, usually allowed me to have a sip of her brandy or cream liqueurs. The adults would spend the evening outside laughing, catching up, telling jokes (Papi's specialty) while we kids were able to play outside until well past our bedtime. We would ride bikes down the street, play volleyball, or start a game of tag—enjoying the thrill of running free all night! We had so much fun together.

These days we are the parents and we continue to enjoy coming together as a family to feast on delicious comida, sip on cocktails, and celebrate *todo lo bonito de nuestra famila*. Slowly over the years with the support of my patient mother, I learned to perfect her recipes, pushed myself to experiment with new ingredients, and became the official party planner of the family. With each new fiesta, party, or celebration, I find myself drawing from my Latin roots and the beautiful and varied countries that make up all that is Latin to inspire me.

From Cuba's vibrant Mojito, Brazil's sweet Caipirinha, or my personal favorite, Mexico's beloved Margarita, these are the colors, flavors, and tastes that run through my veins. With *Latin Twist* I hope to inspire you, whisk you away to new countries, and introduce you to the beauty of all that my Latin roots offer.

Vianney

MEXICO

paloma

pineapple daiquiri

CUBA

DOMINICAN REPUBLIC

GUATEMALA

HONDURAS

PUERTO RICO

EL SALVADOR

NICARAGUA

COSTA RICA

VENEZUELA

caipirinha

PANAMA

COLOMBIA

ECUADOR

PERU

SPAIN

BOLIVIA

BRAZIL

ARGENTINA

CHILE

fernet con cola

borgoña

ARGENTINA
- Wine
- Fernet
- Fernet con Cola

BOLIVIA
- Singani (grape pomace brandy)
- Chuflay

BRAZIL
- Cachaça (sugar cane spirit)
- Caipirinha cocktail

CHILE
- Wine
- Borgoña (wine punch)
- Pisco Sour

COLOMBIA
- Aguardiente (anise-flavored brandy)
- Aguardiente Sour

COSTA RICA
- Cacique Guaro
- Pura Vida cocktail

CUBA
- Rum
- Mojito
- Pineapple Daiquiri

DOMINICAN REPUBLIC
- Rum
- Pineapple-Basil Guarapo Cooler

ECUADOR
- Aguardiente
- Espiritu del Ecuador
- Andean Sunrise
- Rosero Quiteño Punch

EL SALVADOR
- Vodka
- Nance Liqueur
- Coco Loco

GUATEMALA
- Aged Rum
- Quetzalteca Rosa de Jamaica (Hibiscus Flower Liqueur)
- Rosa de Jamaica Cooler
- Spiced & Spiked Coconut Coffee

HONDURAS
- Rum
- Aguardiente
- Coco Rosa
- Honduran Rompopo

MEXICO
- Tequila
- Mezcal
- Beer
- Classic Paloma

NICARAGUA
- White Rum
- Chicha (Moonshine)
- El Macua

PANAMA
- Seco (Brandy)
- Rum
- Tequila
- The Lord Panama
- Panama Red

PERU
- Pisco (Grape Brandy)
- Pisco Sour

PUERTO RICO
- Rum
- Piña Coladas

SPAIN
- Wine
- Sangria

VENEZUELA
- Rum
- El Ritual
- Spiked Papelón con Limón

LIQUOR / WINE / BEER

NATIONAL COCKTAIL

*We are not mixologists or bartenders,
and do not use fancy bartending equipment for our recipes.
The tools we use are very basic, but essential to make any of the cocktails
in this book. We'll show you that you can host a party and have a successful
cocktail night using everyday kitchen gadgets you already own.*

Cocktail Shaker & Bar Spoon

If you'd like to begin stocking your home bar we suggest investing in a cocktail shaker and bar spoon, but believe us when we say a Mason jar and a long spoon work just as well.

Measuring Cups & Measuring Spoons

No need to get fancy measuring jugs—a standard 8-ounce measuring cup, a 1-ounce shot glass, a standard 1.5 ounce shot glass, and standard measuring spoons are all you need.

Blender

To make a frothy cocktail, crush ice, or liquefy pineapple, you'll need a blender. We have a handful of recipes that require a blender, and you'll want to be sure you have one with a strong motor and sharp blades.

Pitchers & Punch Bowls

An assortment of pitchers, carafes, and punch bowls are always nice to have, especially for our wine cocktails. Make a big batch and you'll have something ready to pour as guests arrive. Plus they can help themselves to refills, leaving you free to enjoy your party.

Muddler

A muddler is used for crushing sugar or mint leaves, and particularly useful when making Mojitos. Don't have one? Don't worry—a wooden spoon or firm silicone spatula can be used in place of a muddler.

Strainer & Cheesecloth

A wire mesh strainer that you use in the kitchen works just fine for recipes that involve straining or separating. Some cocktails will also require cheesecloth for fine straining.

Sharp Knife

We believe the easiest way to improve your cocktails is to use homemade mixers and freshly squeezed juices. A sharp knife will be needed to cut all those lovely fruits.

Citrus Juicer

Fresh fruit juices will need a little effort on your part, and a standing citrus juicer or hand-held citrus squeezer can handle this task. No need to invest in an expensive juicer.

Grater

A fine grater, such as a microplane, for grating fresh canela (cinnamon) over Ponche de Chocolate is quite lovely. If this sounds too fancy, then buy ready-ground cinnamon. It's almost as good.

Wire Whisk

An ordinary balloon whisk will do the trick when it comes to whisking eggs for a little frothy texture or whisking milk for some of the creamy dessert cocktails.

Corkscrew

You'll need a corkscrew to open up wine bottles, but something tells us you might already own one.

Zester

A zester is very handy if you already own one, but not needed. We used a simple vegetable peeler and sharp knife for some of our garnishes.

Cocktail Sticks

Cocktail sticks or stirrers are not only decorative, but they can be used for holding ingredients such as olives for a Bloody Maria.

Glasses

We are both addicted to shopping antique stores and garage and estate sales for unique glassware. There is no need to purchase entire sets of cocktail glasses. Buy one or two here and there to start your collection. Have fun serving cocktails in a variety of pretty glasses.

Garnishes

Garnishes make the drink. Can you imagine wearing a fancy cocktail dress but neglecting to put on earrings? The edible extras add color, flavor, and, of course, visual interest to any cocktail. After juicing, use the lemon or orange peels for twists and reserve extras for lemon wheels and lime wedges. But remember, less is more, so do not over-garnish a cocktail.

SIMPLE SYRUP

MAKES 1/2 CUP

½ cup granulated sugar
½ cup water

Combine sugar and water in a small saucepan. Bring to a boil over medium-high heat, stirring, until all sugar dissolves. Remove from heat; transfer to a bowl and chill.

MAKE AHEAD

Can be refrigerated and kept for 3 weeks.

HOMEMADE SWEET-AND-SOUR MARGARITA MIX

MAKES 7 CUPS

3 cups water
3 cups granulated sugar
2 cups fresh lemon juice
2 cups fresh lime juice

Combine water and sugar in large saucepan. Stir over medium heat until sugar dissolves. Bring to a boil. Cool syrup.

Mix sugar syrup, lemon juice, and lime juice in pitcher. Chill until cold.

MAKE AHEAD

Can be made 1 week ahead. Cover and keep chilled.

HOMEMADE COCONUT MILK

*MAKES **4** CUPS*

1 (8-ounce) package unsweetened shredded coconut
4 cups hot filtered water

Combine shredded coconut with hot water in a blender and blend until creamy. Line a bowl with dampened cheesecloth. Pour coconut milk into the cheesecloth and squeeze out any excess liquid.

‹E AHEAD

Store in a mason jar in your refrigerator for up to 1 week. Homemade coconut milk will separate. Shake before use.

*When fresh coconut milk is required, but not available, use a BPA-free can of unsweetened coconut milk. Shake can vigorously before opening. Pour coconut milk into a bowl, and let stand for several hours. Then squeeze through cheesecloth.

MEXICO

Frida Kahlo, the famed Mexican painter, once said, "Fruits are like flowers: they speak to us in a provocative language and teach us things that are hidden." Like Mexico, this chapter is vibrant and full of exotic and tropical fruit cocktails. You might notice that this chapter has a few more drinks than the others. We may be a little biased being of Mexican descent— we've got too many favorites. If you are hosting a Mexican fiesta, these party-perfect drinks will keep the celebration going.

When you think of Mexico, you might think of hard-to-swallow tequila shots or a bottle of mezcal with a worm at the bottom. Once only a drink for bandits and cowboys, tequila and mezcal are now trendy. While plenty have sampled tequila in the form of a Margarita, we have included it in other cocktails that you will love. When it comes to tequila, no need to pick up a saltshaker or limes—relax and enjoy it in one of these cocktails or straight, sip by sip.

SERRANO-INFUSED TEQUILA

Make your own pepper-infused tequila with any tequila you want as long as it's 100% agave.

MAKES *1* BOTTLE

1 bottle (750 ml) silver tequila
2 serrano chiles

Place two serrano chiles inside a bottle of tequila and let steep for 2 days. Gently shake daily.

After 2 days, remove serrano chiles and refrigerate the tequila.

SANGRITA

Sangrita (meaning "little blood") is not the Spanish wine sangria.
Sangrita is a non-alcoholic traditional companion to tequila.
Our version is chased with a fiery dose of spicy tequila.

MAKES **4**

2 medium cucumbers, each about 1½ inches in diameter

⅛ teaspoon ancho chili powder

½ cup fresh orange juice

½ cup clam juice

2 tablespoons fresh lime juice

1 tablespoon minced onion

½ teaspoon Jugo Maggi

Salt and freshly ground pepper

Cut two 3½-inch lengths from each of the cucumbers to use as
cups. Peel the pieces, leaving a 1½-inch band of peel at one end
of each. Using a small measuring spoon, scoop out the seeds,
stopping just before reaching the bottom. Refrigerate the cups for
at least 10 minutes.

In a mason jar or cocktail shaker, place the chili powder, orange
juice, clam juice, lime juice, minced onion, and Jugo Maggi
seasoning and shake well. Strain through a coarse sieve. Season
the Sangrita with salt and pepper and chill for 20 minutes.

Pour the Sangrita into the cucumber cups and enjoy with Serrano-
Infused Tequila (page 14).

MAKE AHEAD

The Sangrita can be refrigerated overnight.

SANGRIA MEXICANA

Instead of traditional Spanish Sangria made with brandy, we add tequila—our favorite liquor. We are both of Mexican descent and we always have tequila in our homes. We combined that with our love of wine and then mixed in our favorite fruits for a Mexican twist!

MAKES **15** SERVINGS

2 bottles red wine (recommend Rioja)
2 cups silver tequila
1 cup freshly squeezed orange juice
1 orange, sliced
1 lemon, sliced
1 lime, sliced
1 apple, cored and cut into thin wedges
1 pear, cored and cut into thin wedges
3 cups lemon-lime soda, chilled

Combine the wine, tequila, orange juice, and fruits in a large container or glass pitcher. Cover and chill completely, at least 1 to 2 hours or overnight.

Add soda to mixture when ready to serve. Serve in glasses with ice and some of the fruit.

MAKE AHEAD

This beautiful drink is best when prepared a day in advance.

MEZCAL PALOMA

Paloma (Spanish for "dove") is perhaps the most refreshing cocktail ever created. Sweet, sour, a little bitter, and salty, it's got all four taste groups, plus ice, bubbles, and tequila or mezcal; what's not to like? We love this refreshing Margarita with bubbles.

MAKES *1*

Coarse salt
¼ cup fresh grapefruit juice
1 tablespoon fresh lime juice
1 teaspoon granulated sugar
¼ cup mezcal or tequila
¼ cup club soda
Grapefruit wedge, for garnish

Rub rim of an 8-ounce glass with a grapefruit wedge. Pour some coarse salt out onto a plate and rub the rim of the glass in the salt to coat. Combine grapefruit juice, lime juice, and sugar in prepared glass; stir until sugar is dissolved. Stir in mezcal, add some ice, and top off with the club soda. Garnish with grapefruit wedge.

photo p. 21

CLASSIC MARGARITA

If we could survive on one cocktail it would be a Margarita. But not made with that fake mix from a bottle! These ingredients are fresh and simple. Since the principal flavor of the Margar. is the tequila, it's important to make sure you've got the best stuff you can get your hands on. Serve it on the rocks with salt like you see here, or serve it up in a chilled glass if you prefer.

MAKES **1**

Coarse salt
1½ ounces tequila (reposado or añejo)
1 ounce Triple Sec or Cointreau
½ ounce fresh lime juice
1 very thin lime slice, for garnish

Moisten rim of a Margarita glass with a lime and coat with salt. Fill the glass with ice.

Pour the tequila, Triple Sec, and lime juice into a cocktail shaker and fill the shaker halfway with ice. Shake vigorously until the outside of the shaker turns frosty. Strain the Margarita into the prepared glass and garnish with a lime slice.

PITCHER OPTION

MAKES **4** SERVINGS

³/₄ cup tequila (reposado or añejo)
½ cup fresh lime juice (from 4 to 6 limes)
½ cup Triple Sec or Cointreau
½ cup water
1 lime, sliced
Coarse salt (optional)

In a medium pitcher, combine the tequila, lime juice, Triple Sec, and water. If desired, rub the rims of 4 glasses with a lime slice and dip in salt to coat. Serve the Margaritas in the prepared glasses over ice and garnish with the lime slices.

CHELADA

Mexican beer and fresh lime juice—it doesn't get any easier than that.

MAKES **1**

Coarse salt
¼ cup ice
¼ cup fresh lime juice
1 bottle (12 ounces) Mexican beer (recommend Dos XX or Tecate)

Moisten rim of a beer glass with a lime. Pour some coarse salt out onto a plate and rub the rim of the glass in the salt to coat. Put ice and lime juice in glass. Pour in beer and drink before the ice melts.

CHAVELA

A classic Mexican prepared beer made with clam juice, the Chavela is sometimes called a Clamato y Cerveza, a Chabela, or an Ojo Rojo.

MAKES **1**

Lemon wedge
Coarse salt
3 ounces clam-tomato juice (recommend Clamato)
Hot sauce, to taste
1 (12 ounce) bottle light-bodied Mexican beer, like Pacifico or Sol
1.5 ounces tequila (optional)

Rub the lemon wedge around the rim of a beer glass; reserve the lemon wedge. Pour some coarse salt out onto a plate and rub the rim of the glass in the salt to coat. Fill the glass with ice; add clam-tomato juice, hot sauce, and beer to fill. Drop in the lemon wedge.

Serve with a shot of tequila, if you like.

SPICY MICHELADA

*The perfect beer cocktail, a Michelada is tangy and spicy.
It is served in a chilled, Tajin-rimmed glass. A tray of Micheladas
would be a hit at a bachelor or Super Bowl party.*

MAKES **1**

Tajin fruit seasoning
¼ cup ice
Juice of 1 lime
½ cup tomato or vegetable juice (recommend V8)
Dash Worcestershire sauce
Dash hot sauce of your choice
1 bottle (12 ounces) amber beer of your choice
Celery stalk, for garnish (optional)

Moisten rim of a beer glass with a lime wedge. Pour some Tajin
fruit seasoning out onto a plate and rub the rim of the glass in the
seasoning to coat.

Put ice in glass. Pour lime juice, tomato juice, Worcestershire, hot
sauce, and beer into the prepared glass and stir. Garnish with a
celery stalk. Enjoy before the ice melts.

TWIST IT

Tajin is a simple seasoning made from salt, chile peppers, and
dehydrated lime juice. You can find it at most grocery stores or any
Hispanic market. We love it as a zesty alternative to a plain salt rim.

TEQUILA SUNRISE

*Tasty day or night, this cocktail is vibrant and colorful like Mexico.
Pour the ingredients slowly over ice or you will lose the sunrise effect,
the grenadine should slowly sink to the bottom of the glass. Make a
Tequila Sunrise with good-quality tequila for a gentle flavor.*

MAKES *1*

1½ ounces blanco or reposado tequila
½ cup cold, fresh orange juice
Splash of grenadine

Fill a highball glass with ice. Slowly pour the tequila over the ice,
followed by the orange juice. Drizzle in the grenadine and enjoy the
sunrise magic.

PONCHE NAVIDEÑO

Ponche Navideño (Mexican Christmas Fruit Punch) is a hot punch served with or without alcohol during the holiday season and most generally during Las Posadas. On those chilly nights this fragrant infusion warms you from the inside out. The intoxicating aroma and perfumed air in your home will certainly entice your guests to give the drink a try. After that, they're hooked. Brandy or tequila can be added, making it Ponche con Piquete (punch with a sting).

MAKES **20** SERVINGS

16 cups water
2 cinnamon sticks
8 whole cloves
5 long tamarind pods, husk removed, and seeded
½ pound tejocotes or crab apples, left whole
6 large guavas, peeled and diced
2 red apples (of your choice), peeled, cored, and diced
1 pear (of your choice), peeled, cored, and diced
2 (4-inch) sugarcane sticks, peeled and diced
1 cup pitted prunes
½ cup dark raisins
1 orange, sliced
8 ounces piloncillo, chopped, or 1 cup dark brown sugar
1 ounce brandy or tequila per cup (optional)

Place the water, cinnamon sticks, cloves, tamarind pods, and tejocotes or crab apples in a large pot. Bring to a boil over high heat. After it starts to boil, lower the heat and simmer for about 10 minutes, until the tejocotes are soft.

Remove the tejocotes or crab apples from the pot with a slotted spoon, peel, remove hard ends, cut in half, and deseed. Return them to the pot.

Add the guavas, apples, pear, sugarcane, prunes, raisins, orange slices, and piloncillo. Simmer for at least 30 minutes, stirring gently. Discard cinnamon sticks and cloves.

To serve, ladle into coffee cups or mugs, making sure each cup gets some chunks of fruit. If desired, add 1 ounce of brandy or tequila to each cup.

TEPACHE

Tepache is a refreshing yet complex drink that Mexican street vendors serve on sweltering days. Tepache utilizes the flesh and rind of pineapples, and is typically sweetened with brown sugar or piloncillo. Even though Tepache is a fermented drink, it does not have a high alcohol content.

MAKES *8-10* SERVINGS

1 whole ripe pineapple
8 ounces piloncillo, cut in pieces, or 1 cup dark brown sugar
1 cinnamon stick
3 whole cloves
16 cups water

Wash the outside of the pineapple thoroughly with a clean brush. Using a sharp knife, cut the whole pineapple into cubes.

In a large glass pitcher, place the chopped pineapple, piloncillo or brown sugar, cinnamon stick, cloves, and water. Stir to combine.

Cover the pitcher or glass container with cheesecloth or plastic wrap in a loose manner that allows the brew to breath. Place this container on your countertop and let it sit for 12 to 24 hours.

With a wooden spoon, remove the white foam that has formed on top of the liquid. Loosely cover again and let rest for another 24 to 36 hours. (Do not let it ferment longer unless you need pineapple vinegar.)

Strain the liquid through a fine mesh sieve into another glass pitcher. Discard the solids. Taste Tepache for sweetness and add more sugar if needed. Serve poured over ice.

MAKE AHEAD

Tepache can be made ahead and refrigerated in a glass container for up to one week.

MEXICO LINDO

You won't feel blue with this cocktail. Serve this festive drink for a summer fiesta.

MAKES *1*

1.5 ounces tequila
Juice of ½ lemon
Splash of Curaçao (½ ounce)

Combine all ingredients in a shaker with ice, strain, and serve in a martini glass. Garnish with a cherry.

BLOODY MARIA WITH SERRANO-INFUSED TEQUILA

A traditional Bloody Mary is a popular complex cocktail containing vodka. This variation goes south of the border and is made with serrano chile-infused tequila. Trust us, this drink is a magical potion to cure a hangover.

MAKES **4**

1 cup Serrano-Infused Tequila (page 14)
2 cups tomato or vegetable juice (recommend V8)
½ teaspoon Worcestershire sauce
½ teaspoon hot sauce of your choice
½ teaspoon coarse salt, plus additional for rims
½ teaspoon ground black pepper
4 teaspoons pickle juice
Juice of 2 limes
4 celery heart sticks with leafy tops, for garnish
4 large green olives

Rub the rim of four highball glasses with a lime wedge. Pour some coarse salt out onto a plate and rub the rims of the glasses in the salt to coat. Fill glasses with ice.

Place all of the ingredients except the celery sticks and olives in a large cocktail shaker along with some ice. Shake to combine, and then strain over the fresh ice in the prepared highball glasses. Garnish with the celery stalks and olives.

CUBA

This little island in the Caribbean is a treasure of tradition and history, still reflected in its cities, architecture, people, and cocktails. Cuba's signature cocktails are enjoyed around the world now. From 1939 to 1960, Ernest Hemingway resided in Cuba, which influenced his prize-winning book, *The Old Man and the Sea*, and where he enjoyed his fill of Mojitos.
The Cuba Libre, said to have been invented in Havana during the Spanish-American War, is a widely popular cocktail in the United States. We personally love Cuba for its high-quality rums and delicious cuisine. Look for a few Latin twists in this chapter featuring one of our favorite spirits.

CUBA LIBRE

The Cuba Libre ("Free Cuba") is a simple cocktail made of soda, lime, and white rum—similar to a Rum and Coke, but with the addition of lime juice.

MAKES **1**

Juice of ½ lime
2 ounces white rum
1 (12-ounce) cola soda (recommend Coca-Cola)

Squeeze the juice of half a lime into a tall glass. Add ice and pour in the rum and enough cola soda to fill the glass. Stir briefly.

PINEAPPLE DAIQUIRI

Like Margaritas and Martinis, Daiquiris are available in virtually any flavor these days. They are almost always made with rum, lime juice, and a sweet fruit—all blended to perfection. This variation includes pineapple, making this cocktail a delicious porch sipper for the summer. Ripe pineapple makes all the difference.

MAKES **2**

1 cup diced ripe fresh pineapple
2 tablespoons granulated sugar
Juice of ½ lime
1 teaspoon maraschino liqueur
About 1 cup crushed ice*
2 ounces rum

Place all the ingredients in a blender and blend until smooth. Pour into two cocktail glasses and enjoy.

*Tip: Fill your glass with crushed ice first to measure the right amount of ice needed for one drink.

BERRY MOJITO

The Mojito (pronounced moe-hee-toe) is Cuba's most famous cocktail.
This berry version of the Cuban classic is maravilloso! Be gentle when you muddle
the berries and mint. You want to release their fresh essence without crushing them so
much that they become bitter. If you don't have a muddler, just use a wooden spoon or
firm silicone spatula. Fresh seasonal berries give these Mojitos a delightful flavor
and beautiful color. Whether you make it with succulent strawberries,
tart blackberries, and/or sweet raspberries, this drink is delightfully refreshing!

MAKES 1

12 mint leaves
3 blackberries
3 raspberries
1 strawberry
2 ounces fresh lime juice
1 teaspoon powdered sugar
½ teaspoon granulated sugar
½ cup crushed ice
2 ounces white rum
2 to 3 ounces club soda, chilled
1 lime wedge, for garnish
Mint sprig, garnish

Place the mint leaves in a highball glass and add the berries, lime juice, and sugars and gently muddle with a wooden spoon or muddler.

After muddling, add crushed ice and rum, and top off with club soda. Garnish with a lime wedge and a mint sprig.

DOMINICAN REPUBLIC

Famous for its pristine beaches, hospitable people, and enticing food, the Dominican Republic is paradise on earth and one of the most popular Caribbean destinations for tourists. This Caribbean island is brimming with tranquil shores, rainforests, and waterfalls. The weather helps to produce the best sugarcane in the world, which makes the smooth rum for which the Dominican Republic is known. One of their most popular drinks is named the Morir Soñando (die dreaming). That says it all!

Caribbean nations are very loyal to their locally produced rums. You hardly ever see someone drinking a rum from another island or country. When dining out, whole bottles of rum are served at the table as wine would be served in other countries, and there is usually none left over!

PONCHE DE FRUTAS CON RUM

This festive rum punch, brimming with fresh fruit and juices, is usually served in a punch bowl at birthdays, weddings, and local festivals. Stimulating, summery, and very smooth, this cocktail will transport you to the Caribbean in a heartbeat.

MAKES **10-12** SERVINGS

4 cups fresh pineapple juice
4 cups fresh orange juice
Juice and zest of 1 lime
1 cup granulated sugar
2 cups diced pineapple
2 apples, diced
2 cups diced mango
1 cup cherries, pitted and halved
1 cup diced pear
1 cup rum

In a large punch bowl whisk together fruit juices, zest of lime, and sugar until sugar is completely dissolved. Stir in fruit and chill for 2 hours.

When ready to serve, stir in rum. Serve in small glasses with a spoonful of diced fruit.

PINEAPPLE-BASIL GUARAPO COOLER

Guarapo de piña magically turns pineapple juice into alcohol. This is a drink that you will crave, especially on a sweltering summer day. Similar to Tepache from Mexico (page 30), this cocktail is very refreshing. The tropical flavors blend beautifully with rum.

MAKES **15-20** SERVINGS

1 ripe pineapple, about 3 pounds
2 cups granulated sugar
16 cups water
¼ cup fresh basil leaves, plus more for garnish
2 ounces rum for each serving
Pineapple ice cubes (page 48)

To make guarapo: Wash the pineapple completely, remove the stem and base and cut the pineapple (with skin) into 1-inch spears. Place the pineapple, sugar, and water in a large pot and bring to a boil. Boil for 15 minutes. Remove from heat, add basil and cool completely. Strain and chill liquid until ready to serve.

To make guarapo cooler: For each cooler, place 2 ounces rum and some pineapple ice cubes in a tall glass and add some of the guarapo to fill. Stir and serve garnished with a basil leaf.

AHEAD

Guarapo will keep in the fridge for one week.

PINEAPPLE ICE CUBES

MAKES *1* TRAY

1 cup pineapple, diced

Place the diced pineapple in an ice cube tray, dividing among the sections. Fill with water and freeze.

PONCHE

*This eggnog spiked with rum is enjoyed throughout
the Christmas season.*

MAKES **6** SERVINGS

5 cups evaporated milk
2 cups sweetened condensed milk
5 egg yolks
1 teaspoon ground nutmeg
2 cups rum

Whisk together evaporated milk, sweetened condensed milk, and
egg yolks in a large saucepan. Simmer and stir over low heat for 10
minutes. Stir in nutmeg and continue to simmer for an additional 5
minutes.

Remove from heat, strain if needed to remove any solids. Stir in
rum and allow to cool completely. Refrigerate overnight. Serve
chilled in small glasses.

MORIR SOÑANDO

Morir Soñando translates "to die dreaming."
This drink tastes like a delicious spiked creamsicle,
and is best made with fresh orange juice.

MAKES *1*

1 ounce Licor 43 or rum
2 ounces orange juice, preferably fresh squeezed
2 ounces milk
1 orange slice, for garnish

Stir ingredients together in a highball glass. Serve over ice, garnished with an orange slice.

TWIST IT

Licor 43 is a Spanish liqueur made from citrus and fruit juices, flavored with vanilla and other aromatic herbs and spices, with a total of 43 different ingredients (hence the name). It is light-bodied and sweet.

PUERTO RICO

Puerto Ricans love a good drink!

Here you will find a twist on the classic Piña Colada as

well as traditional well-known local libations.

All the cocktails in this chapter are rum-based mixed drinks.

If you love rum, then you are going to love this country.

COQUITO

Coconut + eggnog = Festive tropical fun!

MAKES **4**

2 cups Homemade Coconut Milk (page 11)
1 (14-ounce) can sweetened condensed milk
2 cups Puerto Rican rum
4 egg yolks, lightly beaten
Ground cinnamon
4 cinnamon sticks, for garnish

Blend milks, rum, and egg yolks in a blender until frothy; chill.

Pour into glasses, sprinkle with cinnamon, and serve with cinnamon sticks.

PIÑA COLADA

If you like piña coladas and getting caught in the rain then you are going to love this tropical drink. This variation includes pineapple and coconut milk, making for a rich and delicious treat.

MAKES *2*

3 ounces pineapple juice

2 ounces cream of coconut, such as Coco Lopez

1 ounce light rum

1 ounce dark rum

1 ounce Homemade Coconut Milk (page 11)

3 tablespoons canned crushed pineapple

3 cups ice cubes

2 Maraschino cherries, for garnish

2 wedges pineapple, for garnish

Combine all ingredients, except garnishes, in a blender and blend until smooth. Pour mixture into 2 chilled cocktail glasses. Garnish each glass with a cherry and pineapple wedge to serve.

SPICED CHERRY

The delicious Puerto Rican version of the Cuba Libre
made with spiced rum and maraschino cherries
tastes like a cherry cola.

MAKES **1**

1 ounce spiced rum
½ ounce maraschino cherry juice from jar
1 maraschino cherry
3 ounces cola soda (recommend Coca-Cola)
Lime wedge, for garnish

Fill a highball glass with ice. Add rum, maraschino cherry juice,
maraschino cherry, and top with cola. Garnish with lime wedge.

CHICHAITO

A favorite among locals, the Chichaito is not for the faint of heart.
A dash of rum paired with anise liqueur makes a bold,
licorice-flavored shot.

MAKES **1**

1 ounce rum
1 ounce anise liqueur

Fill a 2-ounce shot glass halfway with rum and top with anise
liqueur.

GUATEMALA

The heart of the Mayan world boasts fine aged rums that are
used to create simple and delicious libations. These lovely
cocktails celebrate the traditions and culture of the people.
Tequila is also a very popular drink in Guatemala.

PONCHE DE FRUTAS

This Ponche de Frutas is similar to the Ponche Navideño from Mexico (page 28), but has a few additional exotic flavors such as coconut, plantains, and a hint of ginger. Serve this warm drink at Christmas time.

*MAKES **15** SERVINGS*

16 cups water
3 cinnamon sticks
4 whole allspice
1-inch piece fresh ginger
5 whole cloves
2 (8 ounce) bags dried fruit mix
1 pineapple, husked, cored, and diced
½ medium papaya, diced
4 red apples, diced
1 cup shredded coconut
½ cup prunes
½ cup raisins
3 plantains, diced
½ cup granulated sugar
1 cup dark rum (optional)

In a large pot, bring the water to a boil with the cinnamon sticks, allspice, ginger, and cloves.

Add dried fruit mix, pineapple, papaya, apples, and coconut. Follow with prunes, raisins, plantains, and sugar. Simmer for at least 30 minutes, stirring gently. When the fruit is cooked and sugar dissolved, remove from heat and pour in the rum (if using).

Serve hot with some of the diced fruit.

SPICED AND SPIKED COFFEE

Now this is a kick in the PJ's! A little spice and a little caffeine will definitely get you out of bed on those cold winter days. If you own a French press or regular drip coffee maker, you can make this drink. And if it's a lazy day then add a splash of rum and cozy up by the fire.

MAKES **2**

2 tablespoons ground coffee beans (Guatemalan preferred)
½ teaspoon crushed red pepper flakes
1 anise star
1 cinnamon stick
2 cups water
½ cup Homemade Coconut Milk (page 11)
2 tablespoons honey
Rum (optional)

Combine the ground coffee, red pepper flakes, anise star, and cinnamon stick in a coffee filter set into a drip coffee brewer. Pour the water into the brewer's water reservoir. Set the coffee brewer on to brew. (Or if using a French press, put the dry ingredients in the bottom of the French press and pour in 2 cups of boiling water and let steep before pressing.)

While the coffee brews, gently warm the coconut milk in a small saucepan over medium-low heat. Stir in the honey and continue stirring until dissolved. Pour the brewed coffee into the milk mixture and stir.

Divide the liquid into two mugs and, if using, add a splash of rum.

ROSA DE JAMAICA LIQUEUR

In Guatemala they sell a specialty infused liqueur made with hibiscus (jamaica) called Quetzalteca Rosa de Jamaica. The liqueur is sweet and tart with a burst of hibiscus flavor. This liqueur is poured over ice and sipped in the summertime. We fell in love with Quetzalteca Rosa and enjoy it made into a cooler. The liqueur can be hard to find so we thought it would be easier to make our own. Lucky for us, hibiscus is a Mexican staple in our pantry and so it was easy to recreate.

MAKES 1 LITER

½ cup dried hibiscus flowers (jamaica)
1 liter aguardiente or rum
1 cup Simple Syrup (page 10)

Rinse and drain the dried hibiscus flowers in a large colander.

In a large mason jar, combine the aguardiente or rum with dried hibiscus flowers and Simple Syrup and set aside to steep at room temperature. Once tinted, about 2 hours, strain and discard petals. Reserve liquid and refrigerate in mason jar. Liqueur can be refrigerated for up to one month.

ROSA DE JAMAICA COOLER

MAKES 1

¾ cup Rosa de Jamaica Liqueur
1 tablespoon fresh lime juice
Club soda or seltzer
Mint for garnish

Fill a tall glass with ice. Add Rosa de Jamaica Liqueur and lime juice, and top with club soda or seltzer. Garnish with mint.

PONCHE DE CHOCOLATE

This drink is dedicated to chocolate lovers. When you get down to it, Ponche de Chocolate is essentially chocolate eggnog. This one is deliciously festive for a holiday fiesta but, rich and warming, it's also superb for a chilly day or to indulge a chocolate craving.

MAKES **14-16** SERVINGS

8 cups milk
1 cinnamon stick
6 egg yolks
1/3 cup cocoa powder
Granulated sugar to taste
1/2 cup rum
Ground cinnamon to taste

Bring 7 cups of the milk to a gentle boil with the cinnamon stick.

Separately whisk the egg yolks with the remaining 1 cup milk and the cocoa powder and add to the boiling milk.

Add some sugar and the rum. Stir well and set over medium heat until it comes back to a boil. Serve sprinkled with ground cinnamon.

EL SALVADOR

In this chapter you will find vodka-inspired tropical cocktails.
Vodka is the most consumed alcohol in the world.
Popular for its ease of mixing, it is a Salvadorian favorite too.
And since El Salvador is the land of coffee, we developed
a coffee martini that is sure to have you buzzing.
As the host, be prepared to make a toast before your guests take
their first sip, Salvadorian-style. Salud!

COCO LOCO

Coconuts are plentiful in El Salvador, and it's common to see vendors sell them on the side of the road. A few deft swipes of a machete and the skilled vendor will then pop a straw in the coconut—the freshest coconut milk you'll ever have! Coconut milk combined with vodka is a popular aperitif, and it's quick to prepare when you get an urge to taste the bounty of El Salvador.

MAKES *1*

2 ounces Homemade Coconut Milk (page 11)
2 ounces vodka

Fill a highball glass with ice. Add the coconut milk and top with vodka.

CHICHA RICE WITH PINEAPPLE

A great way to use pineapple peels, this creamy drink is very refreshing.
It tastes similar to Horchata with a hint of pineapple.
Add some vodka and raise a toast to sunny days.

MAKES **6**

1 pineapple
1 cup long-grain rice
1 cup granulated sugar
1 cup vodka

Remove the skin of the pineapple and rinse skins well under tap water. Place pineapple skins in a pot (reserve pineapple fruit for another use) and add water to cover. Bring to a boil and boil until water has been dyed yellow, about 30 to 45 minutes.

Once the water is yellow, remove the pineapple skins and discard. Stir in the rice and sugar. Simmer until the rice is tender. Remove from heat and allow mixture to cool.

Once mixture is cooled, blend in a blender until smooth, adding a little more water if needed. Refrigerate mixture until cold.

When ready to serve, stir in the vodka and serve very cold in chilled glasses.

Note: Use organic pineapple in order to avoid pesticides.

COFFEE LOVER'S MARTINI

Give your java an extra kick—it makes a delicious brunch-time sipper.

MAKES *1*

1 ounce vodka
1 ounce coffee liqueur
1 ounce cold coffee
Three coffee beans, for garnish

Combine all ingredients except garnish in a cocktail shaker filled with ice. Shake vigorously and strain into a martini glass. Garnish with three coffee beans.

NANCE LIQUEUR

Nances are small, round, bright yellowish fruits the size of cherries that thrive in tropical and subtropical climates. In El Salvador they are eaten raw or cooked to make a sweet dessert. El Salvador uses nance to produce a liqueur that is served chilled. Here in the United States, nance can only be found in jars or frozen, but that doesn't mean you cannot enjoy this delicious liqueur. We've put a Latin twist on this recipe using the peel from a lime to perk up the frozen or jarred nances since fresh are unavailable.

MAKES **3** CUPS

6 cups nances, pits removed (if from a jar, drain; if frozen, thawed)
1 cup vodka
1 cup brandy
1 cup water
2 cups sugar
Peel from 1 lime

Place pitted nances in a large bowl and muddle with a wooden spoon or potato smasher. Place in a large sealable glass jar and add vodka and brandy. Seal, shake, and place in the pantry away from direct sunlight to steep for 2 days.

After 2 days, place the water, sugar, and lime peel in a saucepan over medium-high heat and bring to a boil, stirring until all the sugar dissolves. Remove from heat and cool completely. Once the sugar syrup is cool, add to the jar with the nances, seal, and shake to combine and return to pantry for an additional 2 days.

After the additional 2 days, strain the liquid, pressing down to extract all liquid from nances and remove lime peel. Return liquid to sealable jar, store in refrigerator for up to 2 months.

Serve chilled.

REFRESCO DE ENSALADA

This traditional Salvadorian ensalada is a refreshing twist on a classic fruit drink converted to a fabulous cocktail for adults who want to chill out and cool off on a sweltering summer night. Diced fruit, a splash of fresh citrus juice, topped with shredded watercress and spiked with vodka is all you need for the ultimate adult version of a fruit salad. Cheers!

MAKES **10-12** SERVINGS

1 mamey, peeled and diced (optional)
1 small pineapple, peeled and diced
2 green apples, diced
Juice of 1 lemon
Juice of 5 oranges (about 3 cups)
½ cup granulated sugar
1 teaspoon salt
10 cups water
1 cup lettuce or watercress, finely chopped
1 ounce vodka per serving

Place mamey (if using), pineapple, green apples, and lemon juice in a large pitcher. Add the fresh orange juice, sugar, salt, and water; mix well to dissolve sugar. Chill for 1 hour to allow flavors to meld.

Add finely chopped watercress or lettuce and return to fridge. Serve chilled spiked with vodka.

HONDURAS

Honduras is a vibrant lush country that borders the Caribbean Sea and Pacific Ocean. Coconut trees grow all over Honduras, and their fruits are a favorite ingredient in both food and drinks. We've highlighted a few festive and beautiful cocktails that will have you happily sipping the day away as you dream of the ocean views only Honduras can provide. The cocktails in this chapter include coconut milk and rum, true staples of Honduras.

COCO ROSA

Pretty in pink—cool off with this tropical summer drink with a hint of pomegranate. Not only does it taste great, but it would be a beautiful signature cocktail for a bachelorette party or girls' night.

MAKES *2*

Shredded coconut, for rim
2 cups sweetened coconut milk
2 ounces pomegranate liqueur
1 ounce grenadine

Place some shredded coconut on a plate and press the rims of 2 chilled cocktail glasses into it.

Into a cocktail shaker filled with ice, pour the coconut milk, pomegranate liqueur, and grenadine and shake. Strain into the coconut-rimmed glasses.

HONDURAN ROMPOPO

Honduran cooking has a strong Spanish influence with many dishes similar to those of Mexico. This eggnog reminds us of the wildly popular Mexican Rompopo we always have at Christmastime.

MAKES **10-12** SERVINGS

4 cups milk
1½ cups granulated sugar
1 cinnamon stick
½ teaspoon ground nutmeg
8 egg yolks
1 cup white rum

Put the milk in a saucepan with the sugar, cinnamon stick, and nutmeg and heat, stirring until it begins to boil. Remove from heat and allow to cool until just warm.

In a separate dish, whisk the yolks until thickened and pale yellow. Whisk the yolks into the warm milk, then return to medium-low heat and stir constantly until thick, without allowing it to boil. Pour the mixture into a glass bowl and immediately place the bowl in a larger bowl of ice water and let mixture cool, stirring frequently.

Once mixture is cool, whisk in the rum. Strain through a fine sieve into a jar or bottle. Refrigerate for 8 hours or overnight to allow flavors to meld. Serve chilled.

PONCHE DE PIÑA NAVIDEÑO

No holiday is complete without a bubbling hot punch! This delicious spiced Christmas punch fills your home with its exquisite aroma while it cooks. This aromatic beverage warms you from the inside out on those chilly winter nights. It is the ideal calentito for the holidays.

MAKES **10-12** SERVINGS

3 pineapples, peeled and chopped
3 cups water
3 cinnamon sticks
2 teaspoons whole cloves
2 teaspoons whole allspice
¾ cup granulated sugar
1 cup Homemade Coconut Milk (page 11)
4 cups light rum

Place the chopped pineapple and water in a large stockpot and let stand overnight.

The following day, add spices, sugar, and coconut milk. Boil for 5 minutes. Strain liquid into large pitcher. Add rum and serve hot.

NICARAGUA

Nicaragua is a Central American country approximately the size of the state of New York and bordering both the Caribbean Sea and the North Pacific Ocean. Like in Panama and El Salvador, Chicha is a common drink, but now Nicaragua has a national drink of its own. It is called El Macuá. Before you know it, this thirst quencher will be as popular as Mojitos and Margaritas.

EL MACUÁ

Nicaragua's signature drink is named after a tropical bird native to Central America. This cocktail is strong, fruity, sweet, and a bit tart.

MAKES **2**

2 ounces white rum
2 ounces guava juice
1 ounce lemon juice
2 teaspoons granulated sugar

Shake the ingredients together with some ice in a cocktail shaker. Strain into two glasses over more ice and serve.

COSTA RICA

Walk the beaches of Costa Rica and you're sure to hear the greeting "Pura Vida," Costa Rica's well-known expression meaning "this is the life" or "life is good." Studies show that Costa Ricans have a longer life expectancy than other countries in the world. We think the lush beaches, living the pura vida, and sipping on Cacique Guaro have a lot to do with this longevity. Similar to rum, Cacique Guaro is the Costa Rican national drink of choice.

Cacique Guaro was once thought of as the "moonshine" or "chicha" of Central America. No longer produced in a backyard still, Guaro has taken its place as a cultural institution in Costa Rica. Though it is not easy to find in the U.S., Guaro is available throughout Central American countries. Manufactured from sugarcane juice, this clear distilled liquor has a sweet flavor, but be warned, it also has a high alcohol content so it is mostly used in mixed drinks with soda or fruit juices instead of taken straight in the form of shots.

GUARITA

*If you love Margaritas, you are going to love this Costa Rican
version. Similar to a Margarita in flavor, you'll
want to savor every sip of this sweet-tangy drink.*

MAKES *1-2*

2 ounces Homemade Sweet-and-Sour Margarita Mix (page 10)
2 ounces guaro or vodka
2 ounces water

Combine the margarita mix, guaro, and water in a cocktail shaker.
Shake mixture, pour over ice, and enjoy.

BLUE MORPHO

*Blue morpho butterflies live in the tropical forests of Latin America,
and with wingspans up to eight inches, they are one of the largest
butterflies in the world. This drink, as its namesake, is a vivid iridescent blue
with the addition of blue Curaçao. The bright blue and
citrus flavors make it a refreshing summer cocktail.*

MAKES 1

2 ounces guaro or vodka
1 ounce blue Curaçao
Lemon-lime soda

Pour guaro, blue Curaçao, and a splash of your favorite lemon-lime
soda over ice. Stir and enjoy.

PURA VIDA

*"Pura Vida" means "pure life" in English. There is nothing
more reviving than this cocktail made with Costa Rican cane spirit,
fresh orange juice, and a splash of grenadine.*

MAKES *1*

1 ounce guaro or vodka
2 ounces orange juice
Splash of grenadine

Pour the guaro and orange juice over ice in a highball glass and
add just enough grenadine to give your drink a splash of red.

PANAMA

Did you know that alcohol is cheaper to produce
and import than most soft drinks in Panama?
Popular in Panama are rum, vodka, and tequila.
For the full Panamanian experience, sip on one of these
cocktails as you listen to Latin and Caribbean
reggaeton, reggae en Español.

CHICHA DE PAPAYA

This papaya Panamanian-style drink is an excellent way to quench your thirst during the summer, and is easy to prepare. Traditionally this drink is made with sparkling water or lemon-lime soda, but we made this all grown-up and added sweet sparkling wine.

MAKES **18-20** SERVINGS

2 cups papaya, peeled, seeded, and chopped
1 cup pineapple juice
¼ cup fresh lime juice
1½ cups papaya nectar
2 cups sweet sparkling wine (recommend Domaine Ste. Michelle Brut)

Blend papaya, pineapple juice, lime juice, and papaya nectar thoroughly in a blender. Pour in a pitcher and add the sparkling wine. Serve over ice.

TROPICAL PUNCH

Taste the berry flavors with each sip of this slushy tropical cocktail. Similar to a frozen berry margarita, it's slightly icy and thick—just right for a hot day.

MAKES **2**

1 (10-ounce) package frozen mixed berries
2 ounces tequila
1 ounce orange liqueur
1 tablespoon fresh lime juice
1 cup ice cubes

Place the frozen berries, tequila, orange liqueur, and lime juice in a blender and blend until smooth. Add the ice cubes and blend until slushy.

PANAMA COCKTAIL

Sweet, rich, and elegant, this would make a lovely dessert alternative.

MAKES **1**

1 ounce white crème de cacao
1 ounce brandy
1 ounce heavy cream
Crushed ice

Shake all the ingredients together well in a shaker with crushed ice.
Strain the mixture into a chilled cocktail glass.

THE LORD PANAMA

This refreshing iced tea-based drink is sure to cool you off on a hot summer day.

MAKES *1*

2 ounces dark rum (recommend Ron Abuelo Añejo)
4 ounces iced tea
1 ounce fresh lime juice
Lime wedge, for garnish

Pour the rum over ice in a highball glass then top with iced-tea. Stir and add a squeeze of lime. Garnish with lime wedge.

PITCHER OPTION

MAKES *6* SERVINGS

1 quart of water
6 tea bags
½ cup fresh lime juice
2 cups dark rum (recommend Ron Abuelo Añejo)

Pour 1 cup of water in a small saucepan. Add tea bags and bring to a boil. Remove from heat and cover to steep. Allow to steep for 5 minutes.

Pour tea into pitcher. Add remaining water and stir well to combine. Allow tea to cool in refrigerator for 1 hour.

Add lime juice and rum to tea and stir to combine. Serve tea over ice.

PANAMA RED

The Panama Red has only four ingredients and it tastes similar to a cherry margarita. It is usually served in a martini glass instead of on the rocks or blended, but we like our Panama Red over ice (as pictured). Feel free to serve it either way.

MAKES **1**

1½ ounces tequila
½ ounce Triple Sec
1 ounce Homemade Sweet-and-Sour Margarita Mix (page 10)
Splash of grenadine

Shake all ingredients with some ice in a cocktail shaker and strain into a chilled cocktail glass. If you prefer ice, pour directly into a martini glass.

CAFE PANAMA

Hot or cold, this Cafe Panama is creamy and adds a tropical touch, and rum gives the drink an extra shot of warmth.

MAKES **1**

1½ ounces dark rum
1 ounce cold-brewed espresso or other strong brewed coffee
1 ounce Homemade Coconut Milk (page 11)
½ ounce Simple Syrup (page 10)
1 cinnamon stick, for garnish

To serve hot, place all the ingredients except garnish in a small saucepan over medium heat and cook, stirring, until hot. Pour into a mug and garnish with a cinnamon stick.

To serve cold, add all the ingredients to a highball glass filled with ice. Stir, and garnish with a cinnamon stick.

RUM-SOAKED PINEAPPLE

After a long hard week, a tropical retreat is exactly what you need to take the edge off. Don't worry, we've got you covered. Prepare this rum-infused pineapple on Thursday, and tuck it away in the fridge. On Friday, kick off your heels and sip away your cares as you ease into tropical heaven.

MAKES *1*

1 small pineapple
Rum

Remove top of pineapple with a sharp knife and reserve top. Remove pineapple core. Score as much of the pulp as possible. Using the pineapple as a vessel, fill with rum, return top to pineapple, and place in fridge overnight.

Serve chilled with a straw and spoon.

VENEZUELA

Party like a Venezuelan and drink diverse, complex,
and rich cocktails inspired by the many different
people who call Venezuela their home.
These exotic rum cocktail drinks are so varied that they are
sure to please all the guests at your next party.

LA TIZANA

A refreshing fruit punch often served at birthday parties and family gatherings, or kept in the fridge to enjoy all week, Tizana is great for any celebration. Its vibrant red hue comes from the grenadine. The fruit flavors intensify with each passing day. Traditionally alcohol is not added, but we think this stunning punch would be the talk of your next party with a splash of light rum.

MAKES **24-30** SERVINGS

1 banana, diced
1 Pink Lady apple, peeled and diced
1 ripe mango, peeled and diced
2 cups diced cantaloupe
2 cups diced pineapple
2 cups diced seedless watermelon
1 cup strawberries, quartered
Juice of 4 oranges
Juice of 4 limes
1 (33.8-ounce) bottle club soda
4 tablespoons grenadine
2 cups light rum

Place all the fruits in a gallon-size punch bowl. Stir in orange juice, lime juice, club soda, and grenadine. Chill overnight. Add rum just before guests arrive. Tizana will keep for up to a week in your refrigerator.

TWIST IT

Have adults and children at your party? Then omit rum for a nonalcoholic version and have adults add their own rum to their glass.

COLOMBIA

A coffee powerhouse producing some of the best coffee in the
world, Colombia is a picturesque country flanked by mountains,
beaches, and deserts. Travelers flock to Cartagena to view
the cathedral, walk the old stone streets and relax. If you're in
the mood to party the night away, try aguardiente (fire water),
Colombia's drink of choice. Typically served in shots, we've used
aguardiente to make a few cocktails that
will make you feel like you're just steps away from
the cool Colombian cobblestone streets.

Aguapanela: This refreshing homemade favorite non-alcoholic
drink is found throughout Colombia and nearby countries.
A solid block of sugarcane is dissolved into water and then lime
juice is added for tart zing. You need a little muscle power to stir
the concoction until the sugarcane dissolves, so do what
the Colombians do and make a large batch!

Aguardiente: Of all the South American countries, Colombia
might just hold the record for aguardiente consumption. Their
version is a sweet but strong anise-flavored brandy not too far
off from Greek ouzo. Because Colombian aguardiente is hard
to find, we have used the more common sugarcane-based
aguardiente in the recipes in this chapter so that it can be
substituted with rum.

CANELAZO

A hot beverage with spirits, Canelazo is a favorite in the chilly Andean mountains of Colombia, Ecuador, and Peru. It typically consists of aguardiente (sugarcane alcohol), brown sugar or piloncillo, and cinnamon ("canela" in Spanish). It is often made with the addition of fruit juice and cloves, and the alcohol is optional. Serve this aromatic drink for your next holiday party.

MAKES **4**

3 cups water
½ cup light brown sugar
½ cup dark brown sugar
Juice of 1 lime
1 teaspoon salt
4 cinnamon sticks
6 whole cloves
½ cup fresh orange juice
2 cups aguardiente or rum

Bring the water, brown sugars, lime juice, salt, cinnamon sticks, and cloves to a boil. Reduce heat and simmer for 10 minutes.

Stir in the orange juice and aguardiente or rum. Discard cloves and cinnamon sticks; serve warm.

AGUARDIENTE SOUR

The sweet orange juice and tart lime juice, along with an egg white, make this Aguardiente Sour a refreshing, frothy treat.

MAKES **2**

6 ounces aguardiente or rum

2 ounces fresh lime juice

2 ounces fresh orange juice

1 tablespoon granulated sugar

1 egg white, lightly whisked

In a cocktail shaker filled with ice, combine aguardiente or rum, lime juice, orange juice, sugar, and lightly whisked egg white and shake vigorously. Pour into chilled glasses.

CHAQUETA

"Chaqueta" is the Spanish word for "jacket." A few sips of this hot coffee with aguardiente will make you feel wrapped in warmth. Similar flavors to Café de Olla from Mexico, but with a grown-up kick.

MAKES **2**

---

1 cup water
½ cup piloncillo or light brown sugar
1 cup freshly brewed coffee
2 ounces aguardiente or rum

Bring the water and piloncillo to a boil in a small saucepan. Reduce the heat and simmer until all sugar has dissolved. Mix in the coffee and aguardiente. Serve warm.

HERVIDO DE MORA

Traditionally, this hot Colombian drink is made with pineapple, but our version uses blackberries instead. Hervido is sure to make you feel warm and cozy.

MAKES **4-6**

6 cups blackberries
3 cups water
1½ cups granulated sugar
½ cup aguardiente or to taste

Place the blackberries and water in a blender and liquefy. Pour into a large saucepan and stir in sugar. Bring mixture to a boil, reduce heat and simmer for 10 minutes. Remove from heat and slowly stir in some aguardiente. Serve warm.

REFAJO COLOMBIANO

A summertime favorite, especially for backyard gatherings or grilling parties in Colombia, this refreshing drink is made with a mixture of lager and Colombian cream soda. Refajo Colombiano is usually made with Colombiana, a cream soda with a trace of tea flavor that packs a fizzier punch than your typical cream soda. Check your local Hispanic grocery for this soda, but we recommend using Big Red cream soda if you can't find Colombiana.

MAKES **12-14** SERVINGS

1 liter red cream soda (recommend Colombiana or Big Red)
6 ounces aguardiente
3 (12-ounce) bottles pale lager
1 cup fresh orange juice
Lime slices and orange slices for garnish

In a large pitcher combine cream soda, aguardiente, lager, and fresh orange juice. Serve over ice with lime and orange slices as garnish.

ECUADOR

Ecuador's distinct terrain features a backdrop of the snow-capped Andes Mountains, as well as vibrant, green jungles. Cities like Quito, Cuenca, and Guayaquil are known to be a travelers' delight with friendly people, varied cuisine, and historic charm. We hope to visit Ecuador one day and sip away our days taking in the stunning views.

Aguardiente, distilled from sugarcane juice, is probably the national liquor of Ecuador. Here aguardiente (firewater) is sometimes called "puro" (pure) or "caña" (cane) and lends its molasses-flavored kick to many cocktails. The kind they enjoy in South America is made from cane sugar, so rum makes a great substitute if you can't find aguardiente. Keep in mind that the liquor has a very high alcohol content.

ANDEAN SUNRISE

This cocktail is vibrant and fresh, using only the freshest juices and fruits. Shaken to icy perfection, the Andean Sunrise represents today's approach to the art of the cocktail ... Enjoy!

MAKES **2**

2 ounces fruity liqueur (recommend Espiritu del Ecuador)
2 ounces fresh orange juice
2 ounces passion fruit pulp with seeds
2 ounces pineapple juice

In a cocktail shaker filled with ice, combine all ingredients and shake well. Pour over ice in two tall glasses.

ECUADORIAN CANELAZO

Similar to a hot toddy, Canelazo is a favorite in the cold Andean mountains of Ecuador. The recipe makes enough for a cozy nightcap for you and a few friends.

MAKES **6-8**

4 cups water
1¼ cups brown sugar
8 cinnamon sticks
4 whole cloves
1 medium orange, thinly sliced
2 cups aguardiente or rum
Juice of 1 lime

Place the water, brown sugar, cinnamon sticks, cloves, and orange slices in a saucepan over medium heat and bring to a simmer, stirring frequently.

Once the sugar has dissolved, reduce the heat to low and simmer the mixture, covered, for 30 minutes.

Stir in the aguardiente and lime juice and serve warm.

TWIST IT

Ecuadorian Canelazos are traditionally made using naranjilla ("little orange") juice. Also known as "lulo," this green-fleshed citrus can be found frozen whole or as frozen pulp at Hispanic groceries, but it's very rare to find fresh naranjillas in the U.S. so we omitted them from the recipe.

HAPPY JAPA

This fruity drink won the title "National Cocktail" of Ecuador in a competition in the mid 1980s. Named the Happy Japa, it is made from Brandy Naranja Lima (an orange-flavored liquor) and pineapple and lime juices. It has become a cocktail made for tourists, not very popular with the locals who prefer their aguardiente drinks no doubt, but it tastes good and has a nice tropical look.

MAKES **1**

3 to 4 ice cubes
½ ounce grenadine
½ ounce lemon juice
1½ ounces pineapple juice
½ ounce brandy (recommend Brandy Naranja Lima)
1 maraschino cherry, for garnish
1 slice pineapple, for garnish

Place all ingredients except garnishes in a blender and blend.
Pour into a cocktail glass and garnish with cherry and pineapple.

HARMONY

This love potion is made with Espiritu del Ecuador, whiskey, and lemon juice. Espiritu del Ecuador is a golden liqueur made from exotic fruits. Each bottle contains unique and unpredictable flavors, which make the liqueur taste different every time. It's like a perfect first date—full of surprises, passion, and romance.

MAKES *1*

1½ ounces Espiritu del Ecuador or Love Potion #9
1½ ounces whiskey
1 ounce lemon juice

Blend Espiritu del Ecuador and whiskey with lemon juice and ice in a cocktail shaker. Strain into a cocktail glass and garnish.

ROSERO QUITEÑO PUNCH

This traditional punch from Quito, Ecuador, is served at weddings, baptisms, or other family celebrations. An aromatic infused simple syrup with edible rose petals creates the base of this punch. Cooked hominy gives this punch a hearty bite. Diced fruit is blended to add a layer of sweet texture and white wine finishes it off.

MAKES **20-25** SERVINGS

1 medium pineapple

16 cups water

6 cinnamon sticks

10 star anise

20 whole cloves

16 to 20 edible organic rose petals

1 small papaya, diced

1 cup hominy, drained and rinsed

2 cups naranjilla juice or passion fruit juice

½ to 1 cup granulated sugar, to taste

2 cups strawberries, diced

1 bottle white wine

Peel the pineapple, reserving peel. Cut the pineapple pulp into small cubes.

In a large stockpot, bring to a boil the water, reserved pineapple peel, cinnamon sticks, star anise, and cloves, and simmer for 30 minutes. Remove from heat and add rose petals and stir to combine. Cool completely, strain, and chill overnight.

The following day, place half the papaya, half the pineapple cubes, and 1 cup of the chilled syrup in a blender and blend until smooth. Pour into a punch bowl. Add the remaining diced papaya and cubed pineapple and another cup of the chilled syrup to the punch bowl.

Add the hominy and naranjilla or passion fruit juice. Stir to combine. Taste for sweetness and add sugar by the ¼ cup until you reach preferred sweetness.

Stir in diced strawberries and white wine. Chill for at least one hour, serve chilled.

ECUADOR CAFÉ

Enjoy this java cocktail with dessert after dinner,
or as a pick-me-up at a weekend brunch.

MAKES **1**

Espiritu del Ecuador, or similar fruity liqueur
1 cup freshly brewed coffee
Whipped cream

Add a shot of Espiritu del Ecuador or other fruity liqueur to a cup of coffee and top with whipped cream.

BRAZIL

Carnaval, Carnaval, Carnaval—one of the biggest parties in the world—
has certainly put Brazil on the map. Colorful costumes, parades, and
dancing well into the next morning are hallmarks of the celebration.
Brazilians really know how to enjoy life. With one of these cocktails,
you too can sip away the day with a fresh juice made
from the exotic fruits of Brazil—caju, atemoia, jabuticaba, or jackfruit.
Home to the Amazon forest, Brazil boasts an extensive variety of plant
species and is the world's third largest producer of coffee. But we think
Brazil's best gift to us is the Caipirinha. Made from cachaça,
this drink is one of our favorite go-to party cocktails.

Like white rum, cachaça is created from cane sugar.
While rum is typically produced from molasses (processed cane sugar),
cachaça is made from fresh-pressed cane juice which is unprocessed.
This gives cachaça its unique clean herbal flavor.

PASSION FRUIT CAIPIRINHA

*Brazil's national cocktail the Caipirinha (pronounced ky-pee-REE-nya)
is made with cachaça, sugar, and lime juice. Our recipe adds a touch of
the tropics with passion fruit. The Caipirinha can be sipped at sultry
summertime parties or during the cold winter months; its tropical flavors
transcend all seasons. We used fresh passion fruit for this cocktail, but if you
can't find passion fruit, you can substitute a tropical fruit blend nectar.*

MAKES *2*

2 limes, cut into wedges
4 teaspoons granulated sugar
2 passion fruits, halved
1 cup pineapple juice
5 ounces cachaça

Divide lime wedges and sugar between 2 glasses and muddle.

Scoop the passion fruit pulp with seeds into the glasses. Add
pineapple juice and cachaça, stir and top with ice.

SEE PAGE 144 FOR PUNCH VERSION

BRAZILIAN GROG
(QUENTÃO)

This warm grog is traditionally enjoyed during "Festas Juninas" (winter party), especially in the South Region, the coldest area of Brazil. The combination of citrus and spices highlights sweet and piquant flavors. Serve this drink in a ceramic mug to retain heat.

MAKES **4**

1 cup cachaça
1 lime, thinly sliced
1 small orange, thinly sliced
1 cup fresh orange juice
8 whole cloves
4 cinnamon sticks
1-inch piece fresh ginger, peeled
½ cup granulated sugar

In a large saucepan combine all the ingredients, stirring to dissolve the sugar. Bring to a boil and then reduce heat and simmer for 10 minutes.

Remove from heat and pour into 4 mugs. Evenly divide cloves, cinnamon sticks, and fruit slices between mugs; discard the ginger. Serve warm.

BATIDA DE COCO

*This refreshing tropical drink is adored by coconut lovers and sweet tooths
alike. It is unfussy and very popular in Brazil along with Caipirinhas.*

MAKES *2*

1 cup fresh coconut water
4 tablespoons granulated sugar
2 ounces cachaça or vodka
Shredded coconut, for garnish

Blend together coconut water, sugar, and cachaça in a blender.
Serve over ice and garnish with shredded coconut.

MEDIA DE SEDA

*Media de Seda, literally translating to "silk stockings,"
is another milk-based Brazilian cocktail. This cocktail is
especially recommended for those with a sweet tooth.
This silky drink is very rich and suited for the holiday season.*

MAKES **4**

6 ounces sweetened condensed milk

6 ounces milk

4 ounces crème de cacao

4 ounces cognac

2 ounces gin

Ground cinnamon for dusting

Shake all ingredients together in a large re-sealable jar and chill.

Serve in small cocktail glasses and dust with cinnamon.

CHILCANO

*Chilcano is a refreshing mixed drink made with ginger ale, lime,
and a splash of Pisco. In Peru from January 10 until January 19, they
celebrate Chilcano Week—a week set aside to celebrate Peru's beloved Pisco.
This cocktail dates back to 1916. No one is sure how it originated,
but today it is one of Peru's most popular drinks.*

MAKES **2**

2 ounces Pisco
Juice of ½ lime
4 ounces ginger ale
2 drops Angostura bitters
Lime peel, for garnish

Divide the Pisco and lime juice between 2 highball glasses filled
with ice. Top with ginger ale and add a drop of bitters to each glass.
Garnish with a lime twist.

PASSION FRUIT PISCO SOUR

Passion fruit (maracuyá) is as seductive as its name promises.
Fresh passion fruit would be ideal for this drink, but good-quality
nectar works very well. Smooth and sexy, this cocktail—especially when
served with the right company— is magical.

MAKES **2**

½ cup Pisco
¼ cup fresh passion fruit pulp with seeds, or frozen or bottled
    passion fruit puree
Juice of 1 lime
½ cup Simple Syrup (page 10)
10 large ice cubes (or about 1 cup crushed ice)
1 egg white

Put all ingredients in a blender. Blend until mixture is frothy and the
ice is completely crushed and blended. Serve immediately in small
tumblers.

BOLIVIA

Bolivia is home to the world's largest salt mine located near the Tunupa volcano. The Uyuni Salt Flats (Salar de Uyuni) attract thousands of visitors every year. This salt mine extends almost 11,000 square kilometers and even features a hotel made of salt. Bolivia is also known for its vast jungles, death road (for extreme cyclists), and Oruro Carnival that features 28,000 dancers. Bordered by the famous wine-producing countries of Argentina and Chile, the city of Tarija in Bolivia is making a name for itself in the wine industry. Some of the oldest vineyards in South America are found in Bolivia where grapes are grown from 6,000 to 10,000 feet in elevation, giving the country's wines their unique floral flavor. Originally the grapes were grown to produce Singani, Bolivia's national liquor, but now they are being used to create new white wines and rich and spicy red wines.

Singani, one of Bolivia's most prized liquors, is a brandy made from the muscat grapes that thrive in high altitude in the South America region of Tarixa. The production process of Singani differs from that of wine in that grapes go through a distillation process resulting in a clear distilled brandy. This process, as well as the official minimum 5,250-feet elevation for Domain of Origin (DO), makes it difficult to mass produce Singani. Pisco, which is also a grape brandy, can be used in place of Singani.

CHUFLAY

Chuflay (shoo-fly) is a traditional Bolivian mixed drink served for special events such as weddings, family gatherings, and festivals. Since the ingredients are very affordable and easy to come by, it is the most popular way to enjoy Singani. It would be a simple and refreshing cocktail to serve for your special occasion.

MAKES **2**

4 ounces Singani or Pisco
Lemon lime soda, Sprite, or 7-UP
Juice of ½ lemon
Lemon slices, for garnish

Divide Singani evenly between 2 small glasses filled with ice, top with soda and fresh lemon juice. Garnish with lemon slices.

PONCHE NEGRO

Much like a Cuba Libre, but made with Singani instead of Cuban rum.

MAKES **2**

4 ounces Singani or Pisco
1 (12-ounce) cola soda (recommend Coca-Cola)
Lemon slices, for garnish

Divide Singani evenly between 2 brandy snifters filled with ice. Top with soda and garnish with lemon slices.

YUNGUEÑITO

The Yungueñito is a cocktail inspired by the Afro-Bolivians who inhabit a tropical region in Bolivia where citrus is lush—the valley of the Yungas ("warm land"), hence the name. Made with Singani, simple syrup, and fresh orange juice, this drink is like a Screwdriver that pays homage to the tropics, making it the perfect choice for summer days and boozy brunches.

MAKES **2**

4 ounces Singani or Pisco
1 cup fresh orange juice
2 tablespoons Simple Syrup (page 10)

Put all ingredients in a cocktail shaker and shake well. Serve in cocktail glasses over ice.

CHILE

Chile stretches along the Andes Mountains to the southwestern coast of South America and along this terrain you can view more than fifty active volcanoes. National parks, lakes, deserts, and glaciers all make up Chile's impressive and varied landscape. Spend the day visiting local vineyards in Santiago or visit Valapasriso, a coastal city where the nightlife is legendary. Interestingly, Chile's climate is similar to that of the Mediterranean, making it an ideal place for producing red wine. Also, since it is situated between the sea and the Andes Mountains, the grape-growing season sees warm, sun-drenched days followed by cold, crisp nights. This broad temperature range each day is perfect for developing the fruit's flavor, acidity, and deep, rich tannins for red wine. Carménère, Chile's best-known wine, is used to make Borgoña, which quickly became one of our favorite treats after a long day of mixing and styling for photo shoots.

Chile is also well known for Pisco, the potent South American brandy. Interestingly, both Chile and Peru produce and export this liquor, and for decades, the two countries have argued over which one is Pisco's true birthplace.

BORGOÑA

This popular punch makes great use of some of Chile's abundant fresh fruit. The country's central valleys are home to numerous vineyards, and not surprisingly, that is where this drink was born. Borgoña is made from classic Chilean red wine, such as Carménère, and ripe, luscious chopped strawberries. You can choose to let the fruit steep in the wine and pisco for a while, or serve it right away. You can also use any fresh berries you can find, such as blueberries, raspberries, or blackberries. Nothing says summer like a glass of Borgoña!

MAKES **4-6**

1 cup strawberries or seasonal berries of your choice
1 tablespoon sugar
1 cup Pisco
1 bottle of red wine (recommend Carménère), chilled

Rinse, hull, and slice strawberries and pat them dry. Place them in a mason jar with lid. Sprinkle the strawberries with sugar, cover and lightly shake. Let the strawberries macerate with the sugar for 20 minutes.

Pour the strawberries, Pisco, and wine into a pitcher, stir, and refrigerate for 30 minutes. Serve immediately.

CHILEAN PISCO SOUR

Light, tart, and powerful! A popular Chilean cocktail featuring Pisco, lemon juice, egg whites, and sugar shaken together.

MAKES **2**

4 ounces Pisco
2 ounces Simple Syrup (page 10)
1 ounce lemon juice
1 egg white
Angostura bitters

In a cocktail shaker filled with ice, combine Pisco, simple syrup, lemon juice, and egg white, and shake vigorously. Pour into a chilled glass; garnish with a few drops of bitters.

VAINA

In 1879, Chile fought a war against Peru and Bolivia in a dispute over mines in an area that is now northern Chile (but used to be a large chunk of Peru and Bolivia). We mention this because it was recorded that during the war, the officers drank a cocktail made from sherry, cognac, and egg yolk that they called a Vaina ("scabbard"). This traditional drink remains very popular to this day.

MAKES **2**

4 ounces port
2 ounces chocolate liqueur
2 ounces cognac or brandy
4 teaspoons powdered sugar
2 very fresh egg yolks
Ground cinnamon, for garnish

Shake all ingredients except cinnamon vigorously with ice in a cocktail shaker. Strain into two mini cocktail glasses. Dust with cinnamon.

PONCHE A LA ROMANA

Chileans like to usher in the New Year with a festive glass of sweet, decadent Ponche a la Romana—champagne with pineapple sherbet. This would make a lovely bridal shower cocktail or a non-alcoholic drink for a baby shower by simply substituting sparkling lemonade for the champagne.

MAKES **12-16** SERVINGS

1 whole fresh pineapple, finely diced
1 cup pineapple juice
1 (750 ml) bottle of champagne or sparkling wine, chilled
½ gallon pineapple sherbet
Pineapple slices for garnish
Bitters (optional)

Mix the finely diced pineapple, pineapple juice, and champagne. Chill in refrigerator for 2 hours.

Put scoops of pineapple sherbet in a punch bowl and pour in champagne mixture. Garnish glasses with pineapple slices. Serve with a few dashes of bitters, if desired.

ARGENTINA

Taking pride in its gaucho (cowboy) roots, Argentina is the
second largest country in South America and boasts grasslands,
mountains, tropical forests, and the well-known cosmopolitan city of
Buenos Aires. Located on the east side of the Andes Mountains, the
rocky high-altitude terrain has helped to shape Argentina into
one of the largest wine producers in South America.
This terrain gives Argentine grapes the intense flavor that characterizes
the country's bold, rich wines. Although Argentina has become famous
for its wines, the country has also long produced an Italian herbal liqueur
called Fernet. This bitter-tasting liqueur was initially billed as a
tonic that could help soothe colic and menstrual cramps and
aid digestion. With its purported health benefits, Fernet was even allowed
for sale during the Prohibition era in the U.S. Eventually this fragrant
liqueur was combined with cola and served over ice—
thus was born Argentina's national cocktail.

FERNET CON COLA

*Argentina consumes more than 6.5 million bottles of Fernet each year,
making Fernet con Cola Argentina's national cocktail. Fernet is an Italian liqueur made
from twenty-seven different herbs and spices with a slight bitter taste, but trust us
and take a chance on this beloved cocktail—you won't be disappointed.*

MAKES **2**

4 ounces Fernet Branca
1 (12-ounce) cola soda (recommend Coca-Cola)
Lime slices, for garnish

Divide Fernet evenly between 2 glasses filled with ice. Top with
cola, and garnish with lime slices.

EL PATO

*El Pato was created by Salvatore "Pichin" Policastro, one of Argentina's most famous bartenders. He created this cocktail for the World Bartender Championship in 1954, and dedicated it to Argentina's homegrown sport, pato, which is similar to polo. Policastro's book **Tragos Mágicos** (1955) became a go-to guide for up-and-coming bartenders. A gin-based cocktail with sweet and dry vermouth, Campari, Cointreau, and Kirsch, El Pato is a robust drink. Yet, served over ice, it is subtle and dry with a characteristic bitterness from the Campari. If you enjoy a Negroni, you'll love this complex and refined twist.*

MAKES **2**

2½ ounces gin
1½ ounces Campari
1 ounce sweet vermouth
1 ounce dry vermouth
1 ounce orange liqueur (recommend Curaçao or Cointreau)
½ ounce Kirsch
Orange slices, for garnish

Fill a cocktail shaker with ice and add all ingredients. Shake well and serve in chilled glasses over ice. Garnish each glass with an orange slice.

CALIPSO

*A classic, the Calipso combines pineapple, grapefruit,
and raspberry juices with white rum and maraschino liqueur.
Delicious and refreshing!*

MAKES **2**

2 ounces white rum
1 ounce maraschino liqueur
1 ounce fresh pineapple juice
1 ounce fresh grapefruit juice
1 ounce fresh raspberry juice
Raspberries and cherries, for garnish

Fill a cocktail shaker with ice and add all ingredients. Shake well
and serve in chilled glasses. Garnish with raspberries and cherries.

CLARITO

The recipe is very simple—it's actually just a very strong gin martini with a lemon twist. Whether you consider yourself a martini connoisseur or just love gin, try this classic worthy of discovery and celebration.

MAKES **2**

2 ounces gin
4 dashes dry vermouth
Lemon wedge and twist
Granulated sugar, for garnish

Rub the edges of 2 cocktail glasses with a lemon wedge and dip edges in sugar to coat; chill glasses.

Fill a cocktail shaker with ice, and add the gin and vermouth. Shake well and serve in the chilled glasses garnished with a twist of lemon peel.

CLERICO

Originally made with red wine and known as "claret cup," this refreshing quencher boasts the best of seasonal fruits. These days, many Argentinians make it with white wine, but we prefer this classic red wine version.

MAKES **6-8**

½ cup Simple Syrup (page 10)
¼ cup fresh lime juice
1 cup fresh orange juice
1 red apple, diced
1 pear, diced
3 kiwis, peeled and diced
1 bottle red wine (recommend Cabernet Sauvignon)
32 ounces chilled club soda
Lime and orange slices, for garnish

In a pitcher, whisk together Simple Syrup, lime juice, and orange juice. Add diced fruit, red wine, and club soda, stir to combine and chill until ready to serve.

SPAIN

The Spanish do indeed love wine and are famous for their Sangria.
Oranges and fresh orange juice are frequently used in drinks also,
as they are one of the plentiful fruits of Spain.
Come back to this chapter not only for wine-based drinks but
other classic Spanish cocktails that are simple to make and
will impress and delight your friends.

SANGRIA

Sangria is the ultimate party punch—it's romantic, delicious, easy to adapt, and you can prepare it hours before serving.

MAKES *4-6*

1 (750-ml) bottle red Rioja
½ cup fresh orange juice
½ lemon, sliced
½ large navel orange, sliced
½ cup granulated sugar
½ cup brandy
½ cup Cointreau or other orange liqueur
½ cup water
Mint for garnish

Put wine, orange juice, and fruit slices in a pitcher. Add sugar, brandy, orange liqueur, and water, and stir until sugar is dissolved. Chill, covered, at least 1 hour and up to 24.

SANGRIA BLANCO

This Sangria is made with white wine rather than red, which makes a very refreshing drink. This fruity white Sangria is one of our favorites to serve for spring and summer parties and looks fantastic in a glass pitcher.

MAKES **4**

1 (750-ml) bottle sweet white wine

1 banana, peeled and diced

1 orange, sliced

1 peach, peeled and diced

1 red apple, peeled, cored, and diced

½ cup seedless red grapes, halved

12 ounces club soda, chilled

Pour the wine into a pitcher. Add fruit and gently stir. Chill for at least 1 hour.

Serve in wine glasses with some of the fruit in each glass and top off each glass with some soda.

TINTO DE VERANO

Popular in Spain, Tinto de Verano or "summer red wine" is similar to Sangria but much simpler to prepare. It is usually made from 1 part red wine and 1 part gaseosa (soda). Most often, the soda used is a light carbonated lemonade, of which La Casera is the best-known brand. Traditional-flavored gaseosa can be replicated by mixing lemon-lime soda with carbonated water.

*MAKES **1***

2 ounces dry red wine
2 ounces gaseosa or mixture of lemon-lime soda and carbonated
  water
Lemon slice, for garnish

Combine the wine and soda in a tall glass. Add some ice and garnish with a lemon slice.

KALIMOTXO

A popular refresher since the 1970s, Kalimotxo (cali-mot-cho) is a fuss-free play on Sangria from the Basque region. Red wine with cola over ice and a splash of lemon is not only refreshing but makes for the ultimate afternoon pick-me-up.

MAKES **1**

4 ounces red wine
4 ounces cola soda (recommend Coca Cola)
1 lemon, sliced into wedges

Fill a glass with ice. Add red wine, top with cola, and squeeze juice from 1 lemon wedge. Garnish with another lemon wedge.

ZURRACAPOTE

Zurracapote is a Spanish mixture of red wine and various dried fruits and cinnamon. This cocktail can be served either chilled or warm.

MAKES *12* SERVINGS

Zurracapote Syrup
1½ cups dry red wine
3 cups granulated sugar
6 juniper berries, bruised
1 small cinnamon stick
¾ cup diced dried apricots
¾ cup golden raisins

Zurracapote
Zurracapote syrup (above)
2 bottles red wine
½ cup orange liqueur
2 Fuji apples, cored and diced

To make Zurracapote syrup: In a saucepan, combine wine, sugar, juniper berries, and cinnamon stick. Simmer over low heat until all sugar has dissolved; do not bring to a boil. Remove from heat and stir in the apricots and raisins. Allow to macerate for 20 minutes. Strain and reserve fruit and syrup separately. Discard juniper berries and cinnamon stick.

For the Zurracapote: In a large pitcher or punch bowl, combine the Zurracapote syrup, wine, liqueur, diced apples, and macerated fruit. Chill for at least 3 hours. Gently stir before serving.

GRACIAS

To Colette Laroya and Priti Gress for your enthusiasm in sharing our vision and double-triple thank you for suggesting we stray from our original title choice, wink-wink. To Barbara Keane-Pigeon for having such a keen eye when it came to editing our book. Thank you to the entire Hippocrene Books team for your patience and assistance.

To Jeanine Thurston for capturing our dual styles so effortlessly, as we ran rampant garnishing, shaking cocktails, and prepping the next shot.

To the creative genius Heidi Larsen over at FoodieCrush.com for designing a gorgeous cover and book.

To Melissa's Produce for providing the beautiful fresh produce that made our photos shine and cocktails delicious.

To Amy Doherty for letting us borrow so many gorgeous vintage props from The Pink Attic Cat for our photo shoots.

To Isabelle Kline for that gorgeous hutch that held some of our cocktails for our first Latin Twist fiesta. Here's hoping we can collaborate on many more fiestas together.

To Samantha Bowers Koch and Logan Gillette-Ellis for your hair and makeup talent.

To Julia Kaaren for the beautiful floral arrangements you continue to design for our photo shoots.

To Annette Gonzalez for believing in us and sending us different alcohols to test when it came to developing our cocktail recipes.

To Sonia Carr for introducing me to quality cachaça from your beloved Brazil and for letting us photograph your rare bottles.

To Brenda, Angie, Sarah for letting us ransack your kitchen cabinets for trays, linens, and glassware to borrow for our shoots.

To all the friends and family who sampled our cocktail concoctions. Here's hoping we can continue to share these drinks again with all of you in our upcoming book tour. Thank you for your loving support.

From Vianney:

Thank you to my familia for your infinite support, love, and patience throughout this entire process of completing my first book. Thank you Big Daddy, Chuls, and Pips for your endless rounds of applause, high-fives, and happy dances from my first blog post to today. My heart is full. Your support in Sweet Life from the beginning has pushed me to work harder, leave my comfort zone, and truly embrace this journey. Besos.

From Yvette:

To my mom, Evangelina Soza, who has always been my cheerleader and my best friend. I am forever grateful for your unconditional love and support.

Thank you so much to my family (my three musketeers). You truly mean the world to me and I appreciate all the love and encouragement. To my husband, Bill, I could not have done this without your support. Te amo!

VIANNEY

Vianney Rodriguez is a food blogger and recipe developer who enjoys sharing recipes that are inspired by her childhood memories and her Tejana/Mexican heritage. Her blog, Sweet Life, reflects this identity, and has been featured as one of NBC Latino's "Food Blogs We Love," Latina's Best Food Blogs, and Babble.com's Top 100 Mom Food Blogs, among others. Vianney was recognized as the LATISM 2012 Best Latina Food Blogger. She resides with her family in South Texas.

www.sweetlifebake.com

@SweetLifeBake

YVETTE

Yvette Marquez-Sharpnack is a recipe developer, food blogger, and author who draws culinary inspiration from her Mexican heritage. She is co-author of *Muy Bueno: Three Generations of Authentic Mexican Flavor* (Hippocrene Books, 2012). Yvette has been featured in *Latina*, *People en Español*, and *Cosmopolitan for Latinas* magazines, and the Muy Bueno blog has earned a number of accolades, including finalist in the 2012 and 2014 SAVEUR Best Food Blog Awards. She lives in Colorado with her husband and two children.

www.muybuenocookbook.com

@MuyBuenoCooking